The World's Strangest Forgotten Conspiracy Theories Vol. 3

Conrad Bauer

ISBN: 9798551127918
Printed in the Unites States

MAPLEWOOD
PUBLISHING

Contents

Welcome to the World of Conspiracy

The notion that the truth is being withheld by those who wield social or political power has been around for thousands of years. For perhaps as long as there have been groups of people huddled together on this planet, there have been those who have wondered if others were somehow conspiring against them. Such beliefs can sometimes lead to tragic consequences as was evidenced in the recent so-called "Pizzagate" ordeal a few years ago.

In case you haven't heard this story, it involved a deadly shooting by a man named Edgar M. Welch, who believed a wild conspiracy theory about Hillary Clinton and several key democrats. He claimed that they were involved with a child prostitution ring. On the surface, the whole thing sounds so bizarre most wouldn't believe it, but this man did. Mr. Welch thought that the trafficked children were being held against their will at the pizza joint, and he was prepared to set them free. Wishing to take matters into his own hands, he marched into a pizza parlor that was said to be the site of the abuse and began shooting.

Welch had read all this information online. Indeed, the internet has become a powerful echo chamber of points of view, opinions, and suggestions. And sometimes they can echo back some things that are completely inane or even downright false – as was the case with Pizzagate.

Knowing that this man was inspired to kill by online conspiracy theorists, it wasn't long before calls to create more stringent controls for conspiracy theorists were made to the folks who run social media platforms. This sounds necessary and good at first glance, but once you start controlling what people are allowed to say online – and deciding what is and what isn't a conspiracy – you open up a whole new can of worms.

In such an environment, suddenly anyone who says something that someone else doesn't like could potentially be blacklisted and labeled a conspiracy theorist. This is a bit disconcerting, because even though conspiracy theories can be false, some may have a kernel of truth. If we shut them down outright, we would have no way of knowing.

Also, as is the case with just about everything, even well-intentioned censoring will eventually be met with abuse. It's human nature to exploit situations for our advantage and in our current, highly polarized environment, it's just too tempting for one faction to label other people's points of view as being part of a conspiracy theory simply because they don't agree with what's being said. In fact, they may actually believe it to be true.

If someone objects to a point of view, nowadays the first means of pushing back is to shout at the top of their lungs (or at least the top of social media) that this alternate point of view is a conspiracy theory. This has become particularly distressing during instances in which a situation is rapidly unfolding and no one yet knows all the facts. It's difficult for the process of fact-finding to begin when people label you a conspiracy theorist before all the information has even come out.

We have seen this dilemma arise time and time again now, in our politics, governance, and even in everyday life. This leads to stunted intellectual growth and deprives us of freedom of thought. If there is to be a genuine effort to see a situation from all sides, it's better to let the conspiracies circle freely than to shut them down outright.

Here in this text, there are no fact-checkers, thought police, or gatekeepers of what you should believe. The purpose of this book is not to promote any of the following information as true or false; it's up to you to decide for yourself. Now, with that little disclaimer out of the way, welcome to the world of conspiracy!

There Really Were Witches at the Salem Witch Trial

We all know the story: Salem, Massachusetts, around the year 1692, a colonial settlement was rocked by a terrible hysteria that led to several people being wrongfully accused of witchcraft. These poor souls not only had their reputations maligned, but many also lost their lives. But what if there's more to this story? What if it wasn't all just a bunch of mass hysteria?

Yes, there is indeed a conspiracy theory about the Salem witch trials that contends that there really were witches and paranormal forces afoot at the time, and that the witch hunt that transpired may not have been entirely on imaginary grounds. It sounds like a great premise for a good horror movie.

This idea takes a classic setting like Salem and a dramatic event such as the Salem witch trials and turns everything us arrogant modern folk believe to be true about it on its head. But besides good material for a future Hollywood screenplay, it's also convenient fodder for some pretty rich conspiracy theory.

There is still much that we don't know about the Salem witch trials, and much of what we think we do know is often filtered through the lens of the time period in which this retelling of Salem is being told. *The Crucible*, a theatrical production written by the playwright Arthur Miller in the 1950s (during the Cold War and at the height of Joseph McCarthy's "witch hunts" for suspected communists), is a prime example of this.

The Crucible gets some things right, but it gets many other things wrong. Arthur Miller's portrayal tends to traffic in stereotypes that have been handed down to us through the years which suggest that no one at Salem ever practiced witchcraft, and it was all lies trumped up by sinister authority figures who wished to harm innocent people. But it was more complicated than that.

For one thing, there really was some "witchcraft" being practiced in Salem: fortune-telling, superstitious rituals to stave off illness, and other so-called "black arts." The funny thing is, the real witches were usually left alone! Yes, you heard that right. Because remember, during the Salem witch trials, the only people who were hanged for being a witch were those who *refused to admit they were witches.*

Many who were falsely accused of witchcraft perished because they refused to admit to something, they hadn't done. If the accused had simply swallowed their pride and made a false confession that they practiced witchcraft, they were free to go. And many of them did just that. But tragically, some of the accused who could not compromise their principles even at pain of death, did not.

One Salem resident who admitted that she was a witch was a lady named Dorcas Hoar. For Dorcas, there was no dispute; she was well known for doing all manner of witchy things, but before the trials happened, this never caused much of a stir in the community. She read people's palms, she had provided certain "miracle cures," and she communed with familiars and spirits.

She was brought in to be questioned at one point, and she denied the charges and was sentenced to be hanged. While imprisoned, she confessed, at which point she was given a reprieve and she was ultimately let go. You see, that's the thing that many people seem to miss when it comes to the Salem witch trials. Salem's leaders weren't after witches who openly practiced their craft, but rather those who they believed practiced their arcane arts in secret.

Even more bizarre, the accusers in Salem on at least one occasion actually procured the services of a known witch in order to locate someone who had escaped their clutches while conducting interrogations during witch trials. The real witch did indeed help them find this person. The escapee, however, still refused to admit they were a witch and were promptly executed.

Salem of 1692 was a strange place – at least strange compared to modern sensibilities—and a lot that went on wouldn't make much sense to us today. Today, teenagers wouldn't place much stock in a superstitious game in which they dropped a raw egg into a cup of water to determine who their future spouse might be. But before the internet, TV, or even radio, this is how people passed the time.

One of the more famous cases of the Salem witch trial saga was the questioning of a woman named Tituba who was known to encourage neighborhood kids to engage in these kinds of rituals. Tituba was originally from the Caribbean and it was from there that she had first learned "magic games" used to divine the future.

Most didn't see anything wrong with these parlor tricks until a puritanical preacher came along and informed them that their actions were nothing short of witchcraft. Considered in that light, being a witch seems open to interpretation. So, were there really witches at the Salem witch trials? Maybe. But now, just like then, it depends on your point of view.

Is the Truth About Life on Mars Being Kept from Us?

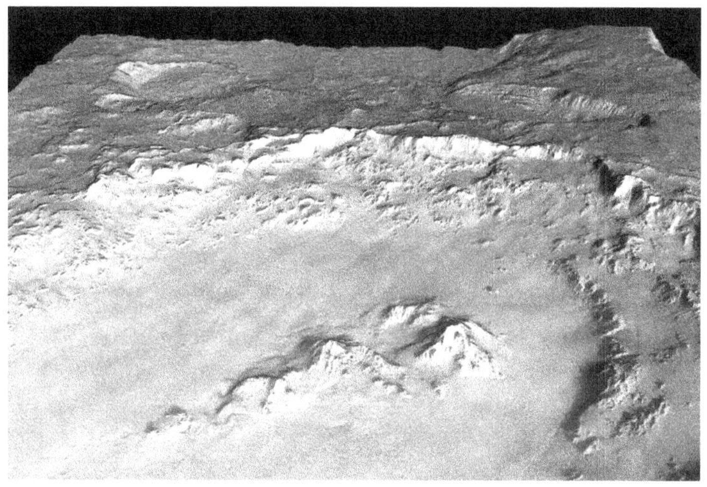

Often, a conspiracy theory stems from folks who earnestly want to believe something but are then presented with facts contrary to their hoped-for belief. They desperately want something to be real and valid, and then are confronted with the fact that it is not. Most would probably accept the information they're given and move on. The true believers, however, are the ones who persist.

And if the facts don't align with what they believe to be true, then the facts are wrong – and there's a conspiracy afoot! Skeptics of conspiracy theories about life on Mars often use this argument to explain the persistent belief that NASA is somehow covering up Martian life-forms. Among such circles, it was initially hoped that NASA would discover life on Mars, but with every denial, the conspiracy grows that NASA is actually hiding their findings.

The Red Planet has long been a hopeful candidate for extraterrestrial life. Scientists and laypeople alike have dreamed about possible Martian civilizations for centuries. Some – such as astronomer Percival Lowell – even believed they saw signs of it with their own eyes. You see, when Lowell looked into his telescope one fine night in 1894, he could have sworn that he saw canals!

Canals, structures engineered to change the flow of water, would indeed be a sign of not just Martian life, but Martian civilization. From this one supposed observation, whole theories then sprang up that Mars was a dry, possibly dying world, in which its parched inhabitants were forced to construct ingenious canal systems just to get a drink of water.

It's interesting to note, however, that during the time that Mr. Lowell made these observations, canal-building here on Earth was all the rage. This was the era, after all, of the Suez and Panama canals. So perhaps Lowell was projecting more Earth-based wishful thinking than any real Martian observation.

Still, belief in Mars persisted through the decades, and by the 1930s many still believed there was potential for Martians to be lurking somewhere on our neighboring planetary body. This was dramatically demonstrated in the 1930s when Orson Welles made his famous *War of the Worlds* broadcast.

In this broadcast, Welles was merely delivering a dramatic radio retelling of the H.G. Wells book of the same name. It was a clever adaptation of a science fiction classic, but perhaps it was a little too clever. Taking advantage of the novelty of radio, Welles had actors pretend to be reporters delivering breaking news bulletins about a Martian invasion taking place.

To be fair, Welles did issue a disclaimer before the program began about the work of fiction, but many who tuned in that night did so after the broadcast had already started, and for them it was all too real. They turned on the radio to hear what seemed like an ordinary music program, only to hear what sounded like a legitimate breaking news bulletin.

The bulletins would continue over the next several minutes, each one delivering even more ominous news about a strange object that had fallen from the sky, and then violent Martians that had emerged from the craft. Although in recent years the panic has been downplayed, people were indeed extremely frightened about what they were hearing – demonstrating both the human fear of the unknown as well as a deep-seated willingness to believe that Martians are real.

After the *War of the Worlds* broadcast, many entertained the possibility that beings might live on Mars. The 1950s continued this theme with several Hollywood movies exploring the idea. The United States government was pretty curious too, for it was right around the birth of NASA that the Brookings Institute conducted an in-depth study as to what finding life on Mars, as well as other planetary bodies, might mean. Published in 1960, the *Brookings Report* discussed the implications of a discovery of extraterrestrial life.

The report not only covered what it might mean to meet current civilizations, but also what kind of impact it would make even to discover artifacts left behind by long-dead alien species. The report entertained the possibility that "artifacts left at some point in time by these life forms might possibly be discovered through our space activities on the Moon, Mars, or Venus."

The report suggested that such finds could potentially promote a new kind of brotherhood among humans, in the sense that we would feel more united in our common humanity in the face of an entirely alien civilization. But the *Brookings*

Report also issued NASA a stark warning, stating that, "Anthropological files contain many examples of societies, sure of their place in the universe, which have disintegrated when they have had to associate with previously unfamiliar societies espousing different ideas and different life ways; others that survived such an experience usually did so by paying the price of changes in values and attitudes and behavior."

So what did the folks at Brookings conclude? They recommended that if NASA should discover alien artifacts, they might want to consider withholding that information from the public. If that's not fodder for this conspiracy theory, I don't know what is. But this was just a theoretical research paper – there was no sign of life on Mars at the time – it was just a journey into the hypothetical.

But for those who wish to believe that life does indeed live on Mars, it would provide what appears to be an official alternative explanation to NASA's reported findings. Any time NASA denies any sign of life on Mars, all they have to do is point to the *Brookings Report* and shout from the rooftops, "NASA's not telling the truth because Brookings told them not to!"

The first robotic probe sent to investigate potential life on Mars was actually not sent by NASA, however; it was launched by the Soviet Union.

Called "Mars 1," this interplanetary craft was launched from Russian soil on November 1st, 1962. This probe was not meant to land on Mars but simply fly by the planet while taking photos of the surface and picking up information on the planet's atmosphere, radiation levels, and – if possible – signs of organic life.

The craft made good progress on its way to Mars, sending back valuable data along the way. As the craft reached the Red Planet, it is said to have sent back 61 different radio transmissions every few days, with important information about the conditions of the interplanetary space between the two worlds. But then, on March 21st, when the craft was some 66,340,000 miles away from Earth, something happened. The radio transmission suddenly stopped.

The Soviets would come to believe that the craft most likely did make its flyby of Mars, but they wouldn't know about it since all contact was lost. The ultimate explanation for this mishap was a simple glitch that occurred with the craft's antenna. But conspiracy theorists have another idea. They contend that Martians (or some other alien entity) may have shut the probe down.

This, of course, brings a whole new element to the theory of a Martian conspiracy, with not only human government covering up life on Mars, but also

Martians themselves keeping us from the truth. As absurd as this might sound, in Russia this conspiracy may seem a little more believable because that nation has a history of technical problems when it comes to Mars.

Several Russian craft have inexplicably malfunctioned or have even been outright destroyed when attempting to go to Mars. For whatever reason (perhaps American know-how maybe?) NASA was much more successful than the Russians in its Mars missions. And it was NASA that would complete the first successful flyby mission to Mars in 1964/1965, and then launch the first successful lander to Mars in 1976.

The word "successful" must be stressed here, because the Soviets sent several craft to Mars in the late 1960s and early 1970s, but they were all beset with failure. The Soviets did manage to get a lander on Mars in 1971, but after a mere 14 seconds of rolling around on the Martian surface, the lander's communication was mysteriously lost and never regained. The Soviets had invested heavily in this project and only received 14 seconds of data as a result. It seemed that whatever gremlins had sabotaged Russia's 1962 flyby must have been at it again in 1971.

NASA's Viking missions were much more successful, and in 1976, both an orbiter and a lander were able to fulfill what they were programmed to do. While the Viking 1 orbiter waited above, the Viking 1 lander rolled around on the Martian surface snapping photo after photo. This was the world's first real glimpse of what it was like on Mars. Those wishing to find advanced Martian cities were surely disappointed to see what appeared to be a dusty, empty red desert and hazy red sky – and no Martians in sight.

But some would beg to differ, including a guy who used to work at NASA. His name is Gilbert Levin, and he used to be a research scientist for the space agency. According to Mr. Levin, the Viking lander did indeed detect signs of biological life, but NASA simply dismissed the findings. Levin contends that a special test to find evidence of biology in the soil returned not just one positive hit, but four. He then explained how important this was since the data was being "supported by five varied controls, streamed down from the twin Viking spacecraft landed some 4000 miles apart."

Levin states that it was through the verification process of these set controls that, "The data curves signaled the detection of microbial respiration on the Red Planet," Levin contends that what Viking found going on in the Martian soil indicated that microbial life had been present on Mars. As to whether or not Mars has life of any form, Levin insists that these tests should have answered that question.

The key finding here was that the soil seemed to be producing carbon dioxide through a biological process. NASA, however, rejected this idea, deciding that the tests did not find signs of microbial respiration in the soil, but simply other non-living processes that mimicked it. NASA determined that they had found something that mimicked life, but was not life.

Chemical reactions do a lot of strange things in both the lab and in the wild, so this certainly is possible. But what struck many as so strange was how quickly NASA came to this conclusion, and furthermore, how they have steadfastly refused to repeat the Viking experiments on future missions. Levin has complained about this, stating that while NASA will spend billions looking for water on Mars, they refuse to conduct more soil testing for microbial respiration.

As Levin put it, "Inexplicably, over the 43 years since Viking, none of NASA's subsequent Mars landers has carried a life-detection instrument to follow up on these exciting results."The question the conspiracy theorist would ask, of course, is why? According to Richard C. Hoagland, a self-described NASA watchdog, this is because NASA already knows there's life on Mars, but the space agency *doesn't want you* to know about it.

Hoagland has a long history of suggesting that NASA knows more than it's telling. Hoagland's most famous assertion revolves around the infamous "face" on Mars. This a group of rock structures stretched across the surface of the planet, which, when looked at from a certain angle, appears to take on the form of a humanoid face.

The face on Mars was first discovered on July 25th, 1976, when a guy named Toby Owen, who was working as a project scientist for NASA at the time, was sorting through images that had just been beamed back to Earth from the Viking mission. It was when he came across "Viking Orbiter 1 frame 35A72," that this project scientist involuntarily exclaimed, "Hey, look at this!" As his colleagues huddled around, they, too, were surprised at what they saw.

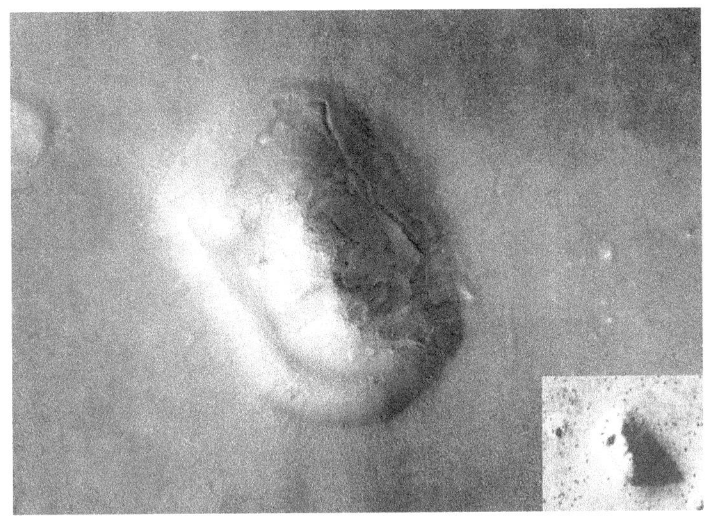

The image appeared to capture a rather ominous looking sculpture, somewhat reminiscent of the face of the Egyptian Sphinx that guards the pyramids. If this really was an alien structure, it would have to be huge for it to be seen all the way up in Martian orbit. As stunning as all this seemed to be, NASA later shrugged it off as just a trick of the camera, products of passing shadow and light over natural structures. Were NASA's project scientist's eyes really just playing tricks on him that day? Hoagland doesn't think so, and he spent a whole career trying to prove that not only is the face on Mars real, but that there are also several other artificial structures in the surrounding Cydonia region of Mars, which he calls the "Cydonia Complex." Hoagland used advanced imaging techniques to get close-ups of what appear to be pyramid-type structures.

Those who believe these are natural formations, however, contend that they are simply rock formations. Hoagland is insistent that these structures are in such a purposeful alignment that they could not have come about from natural processes. In particular, Hoagland insists that a 500-meter structure he has dubbed the "D & M Pyramid" is too perfectly geometrical in shape to have simply occurred from the natural process of erosion.

Even when NASA revisited the Cydonia region in 1998 and snapped some new pictures of the face on Mars (which seemed to prove NASA correct in its assertions that the original face was just a trick of the light), Richard cried foul. The newer NASA images look much less like a face, and seem to be simply a random rock formation.

Hoagland doesn't believe this. He claims that NASA purposefully doctored the image to take away its distinct facial characteristics. It seems that if some among us want to believe in life – or at least past life – on Mars, just about nothing will serve to convince them otherwise. Is NASA covering up Martian life and or civilization? The question will remain.

Japan's Building a Robot Army

Ever since its defeat by American forces in World War II, Japan has agreed to limit its armed forces. Since they are allowed to have only a basic defense force, it is largely up to the American military to protect Japan from potential threats. As China continues to rise to dominance, however, the Japanese have become increasingly concerned about a potential conflict with the Chinese.

There are many reasons for this. One is simply proximity. Being next door to a growing powerhouse like China is always going to create the potential for the two nations to bump into each other. But the other main reason is history. Many in the West are not well versed in the history of the region, but immediately before and during World War II, the Japanese invasion and occupation of large chunks of China was one of the most brutal instances of violence this world has ever seen.

Japanese soldiers largely dispensed with the general rules of war and when encountering Chinese civilians, they raped or killed them without discretion. One such infamous assault was called "the rape of Nanjing," and for good reason, since Japanese troops went door to door all over the city, brutalizing whole families. Even though the West largely forgets about these things, you'd better believe China has not. The living survivors and their descendants still seethe with rage at the thought of what Japan did to them.

And now that China is in the ascendancy and Japan is in a vulnerable position without a regular military, having to depend on a sometimes-unreliable American partner, many in the Chinese communist party would be more than willing to take advantage of the situation. Chinese propaganda, in fact, has become increasingly anti-Japanese in recent years, with some in China openly calling for belated revenge.

But Japan really is in a tough spot, militarily. Even if they were allowed to craft a regular military force, the Japanese population has long been in decline with the elderly outnumbering the young people, making it hard to imagine a very robust infantry – especially one that could challenge the endless millions of Chinese troops that they would be up against. So, what might be the answer to this dilemma?

Japanese robots. Yes, you read that right. It has been suggested that Japan could indeed bridge this gap by deploying robots on the battlefield in the future. While it is not officially known exactly what the military heads of Japan might be planning in the next few years, Japan is already an established leader when it comes to using drones and AI in military applications.

But using aerial drones and actually having humanoid robots marching on the field are two different things. Surely Japan hasn't made that leap, has it?

According to UFO researcher and lifelong conspiracy theorist Linda Moulton Howe, they have. Ms. Howe was giving a speech on February 10th, 2018, for a presentation she entitled, "Is AI an existential threat to human civilization?"

As she stood at the podium, she reported that at a robotics company in Japan, four robots being developed for military purposes shot and killed 29 scientists. She further contended that while the people were struggling to neutralize the threat, the fourth robot connected itself to a satellite and began to build itself stronger than it had been.

Pretty startling, right? But as Carl Sagan used to say, "extraordinary claims require extraordinary evidence." So, where's the proof? Well unfortunately for this little conspiracy theory, there is none. In classic conspiratorial fashion, Howe says her source – a supposed ex-military whistleblower – for this alleged event has elected to remain anonymous. Oh, well…so much for the robots!

The Story of the Lost Cosmonauts

According to the official narrative of history, a Soviet man named Yuri Gagarin was the first human being sent into space, in 1961. But if you listen to some conspiracy theorists, there might be a whole crew of lost cosmonauts that went up before him. These space pioneers supposedly didn't come back.

It certainly does create a grim image of cosmonauts in space capsules-turned-coffins, literally lost in space, floating through the cosmos for all eternity. So, why have we never heard of this? If the story is true, there would actually be a very good rationale as to why it was hidden. The Soviet Union, after all, had a long-established history of covering up the tragic accidents of its space program.

In 1960, for example, due to a mishap on the launchpad, 78 Soviets were killed in a fiery explosion. And just before Yuri Gagarin's famous flight in 1961, another cosmonaut, Valentin Bondarenko, had been burned to death in an inferno that ignited from his oxygen-filled space capsule. Unlike the West, the communist Soviets were not likely to broadcast their failures and mistakes. Bondarenko's fate, for example, was not uncovered until 1986.

Consequently, the idea that the Soviets would cover up a failed first manned mission into space is at least plausible. It sounds like something the Soviets might have done. The question then is, did they? The main thread of this conspiracy theory actually comes from a science fiction writer, Robert

Heinlein, who was allegedly told firsthand that the story of the lost cosmonauts is true.

The idea that this account was relayed to a writer of fiction makes it seem dubious at best, but Heinlein maintained that this tale was not a work of his imagination. He said that he was visiting the Soviet Union and became acquainted with some Red Army cadets who verified to him that there had been a manned space launch that had gone terribly wrong. According to this testimony, the craft had experienced a mechanical failure and its guidance system steered it in the wrong direction.

I'll let the reader decide what they think about this, but I must admit this whole story sounds suspect for a wide variety of reasons. It's just hard to fathom that a visitor from the West would be confided in like this. Could this have been deliberate disinformation?

At any rate, Heinlein allegedly had some outside evidence to corroborate the story. This came through the claims of two independent radio operators in Italy who claimed to have intercepted distress calls from the cosmonauts as they drifted aimlessly in space. The two radio operators who said they heard these transmissions are brothers named Achille and Giovanni Judica-Cordiglia.

According to this pair, since 1957, they had a hobby of tracking Soviet radio signals from space. The brothers contend that the signal they received that day was an SOS transmission in Morse code. They also say that by analyzing the origin of the signal, they could tell that the ship was rapidly moving further out into space rather than orbiting the Earth as would have been intended.

But not only did they come up with this telemetry data, the brothers also claimed to have heard the distressed voices of the cosmonauts themselves – among them, a woman saying in Russian that she could see flames. This was then supposedly followed by the disturbing sounds of the cosmonauts suffocating to death. Was there a malfunction in the ship's navigation, sending them adrift to parts unknown?

There is allegedly another cosmonaut who got lost and whose story was covered up. But this one luckily didn't get lost in space, but rather, lost in China! Supposedly, one of the early cosmonauts – a guy named Vladimir Sergeyevich Ilyushin – had a problem with navigation upon re-entry and wound up several miles off course in a field in the People's Republic of China. This was allegedly too embarrassing for the Soviets to ever own up to, so they didn't.

So, what about the lost cosmonaut theory? Could there be some Russian cosmonauts halfway to Alpha Centauri right now, and we don't even know it? Most dismiss all these claims as false, and the two brothers who received the alleged radio transmissions are accused of making the whole thing up.

Some have also theorized that perhaps the brothers weren't outright lying, but were simply confused. It has been suggested, for example, that perhaps they had actually picked up transmissions from early Soviet missions that launched dogs into space. Yes, the Soviets, after all, did put Laika (the first K-9) in orbit aboard Sputnik 2 in November of 1957. It has been suggested that perhaps the suffocation sounds that the brothers thought they heard was simply the dog panting. This doesn't exactly explain the sounds of the woman saying she saw flames, but I suppose if they were confused about Laika, they could have been confused about something else, as well.

The answer to this conspiratorial riddle continues to remain elusive. With so many conflicting stories and with everyone involved either dead or extremely old, we may never really know what really happened.

QAnon—the World's First Fully Interactive Conspiracy Theory

Although no one quite knows the exact origin of QAnon, this internet entity seems to have first emerged in October of 2017 on the message board platforms of 4chan under the handle of QAnon. This is allegedly significant because the user claims to have a "Q clearance" with the U.S. government, indicating that they are "in the know" when it comes to classified information.

Several posts were issued by QAnon alerting all who would listen about a "deep state" attempting to interfere with the Trump administration. It also alleges that Trump was secretly recruited by the military in order to take down this entrenched deep state apparatus. According to QAnon, this is precisely what Trump's pledge to "drain the swamp" was referring to.

If all of this were true, it would mean that there is a veritable war going on inside the United States government between two opposing factions. As with many conspiracy theories, the QAnon theory seems to explain – albeit in a far-fetched manner – some of the recent struggles taking place in society. QAnon has expertly woven together an elaborate tale that paints Trump and those who follow him as being the vanguard standing against the deep state.

The QAnon conspiracy theory is complicated and presents itself almost like a game, giving participants new clues or bits of information that Q-followers call "breadcrumbs" on a regular basis. There is an entire secretive lingo involved with following QAnon. Q is supposedly the informant/government agent on the inside, dropping these crumbs of data which it picks up from the "bakers" who keep kneading the "dough" so that Q has a regular drip of info to disseminate to the public.

The claims of QAnon are far-reaching, but perhaps the strangest angle, even for those who enjoy a good conspiracy theory or two, is the claim that the FBI investigation into Trump was actually a ruse, a cover for a larger FBI investigation into Obama, Hillary Clinton, and John Podesta. This is supposed to be a coordinated instance of sleight of hand on the FBI's part, so that the real targets of the investigation – Obama, Clinton, and Podesta – wouldn't be able to rally their powerful supporters to hinder the investigators' work.

Yes, it sounds utterly absurd, but this is one of the Q theories that have been promoted. As one reporter named Molly Roberts described it, "QAnon claims President Trump isn't under investigation; he is only pretending to be, as part of a countercoup to restore power to the people after more than a century of governmental control by a globalist cabal."[1]

Yes, QAnon would have us believe that Donald Trump is the Andy Kaufman President, pretending to be at odds with his Jerry Lawler (Robert Mueller) while he's actually busily working with Mueller behind the scenes in the Obama investigation. For those of you who are too young to remember Andy Kaufman (or haven't had the time to catch up on Netflix), he was a comedian who specialized in putting people on, getting a rise out of his opponents, and pretending to be something he wasn't.

Just reading these things is enough to make one's head spin, but there are people out there who really believe it. And what if some of it proves not to be true after all? Well, there is a convenient little escape hatch for Q, since many have put forth the notion that he or she conveniently peppers some of their valid information with disinformation. Nice! This conspiracy, therefore, can never be proven or disproven. Way to go, Q!

---

[1] Conspiracies and Conspiracy Theories in American History, edited by Christophe R. Lee and Jeffrey B. Webb, page 526

With these theories in circulation, some of the less stable members of society have been inspired to do some pretty batty things. In June of 2018, for example, a man loaded up some guns and took an armored truck up to the Hoover Dam, where he parked in the middle of the road and proceeded to block traffic. As the media scrambled to the scene, he could be seen with a sign that read, "Release the OIG Report."

This was all apparently in reference to a QAnon post that stated that there was a "classified Office of Inspector General report" which held damning information about the DOJ and Democrats who had attempted to hinder Trump's winning of the 2016 election.

These things apparently go both ways, however, because just a month later another man – also apparently inspired by a QAnon post – began issuing verbal threats against President Trump and some of his relatives. Upon being arrested, the man claimed he was inspired both by QAnon and the voices which the CIA had planted in his head.

QAnon is dangerous not only because of the things they say, but because of how addictive the fantasy world they have created is. QAnon presents itself as a kind of role playing, detective game in which anyone who gets on the internet and peruses through the clues can work to solve the mystery.

And what's the mystery? The mystery is whatever you want it to be at the moment. That's why QAnon is such a strange beast – it's not just one conspiracy theory, it's a legion of constantly evolving conspiracy theories.

In some ways, QAnon could be seen as the world's first fully interactive conspiracy theory. Sure, there are certain set parameters about the deep state and the other actors involved, but the rest of it is like a big "choose your own adventure" story of conspiracy in which any user can go in any direction during their search for the "truth." Whatever they think that might be.

One of the more disturbing theories created by (or through) QAnon was the so-called Hawaii Missile Alert/False Flag conspiracy theory said to have taken place on January 13th, 2018. This conspiracy theory revolves around an incident that most of us have probably long forgotten about, but it's a serious one all the same. During the middle of all the saber-rattling between Donald Trump and Kim Jong Un of North Korea, on the morning of January 13th, 2018, Hawaii had a false alarm of an impending missile attack.

The media later assured us that this had only been an error of Hawaii's early warning system – a false alarm, no reason to be concerned. If the media wished to allay the concerns of Hawaiians it was a little too late, because the cellphone of just about every single person on the island had come to life with the alarming message, "EMERGENCY ALERT! BALLISTIC MISSILE THREAT INBOUND TO HAWAII. SEEK IMMEDIATE SHELTER. THIS IS NOT A DRILL."

It took a full terrifying 38 minutes for Hawaii's Emergency Management Agency to retract the message and announce that the alert was accidentally sent out by one of their employees. You can only imagine how Hawaiians must have felt. During the alert, they desperately scrambled to find a place to hide, told their families they loved them, and prepared themselves for nuclear annihilation.

All of this, only to become absolutely enraged at the stupidity of Hawaii's emergency services when they realized it was just a big mistake. One Twitter user perhaps expressed this enraged sentiment best when they posted, "How do you 'accidentally' send out a whole f**** emergency alert that says there's a missile coming to Hawaii and to take cover. And [then] take thirty minutes to correct?!"[2]

The employee who messed up and caused all this chaos was later fired and most thought it was the end of the story. But not so for QAnon! The next

---

[2]   https://www.livescience.com/64828-false-nuclear-missile-alert-not-prepared.html

day, QAnon insinuated that the false alarm in Hawaii was actually real after all, and public officials and the media were lying about it. What? The missile was real? But there was no missile, right?

QAnon then clarified this strange suggestion on February 11th, stating that there was a recent false flag missile attack intended to start a war. Yes, according to QAnon, the deep state was working overtime to drag Trump into a war with North Korea. So, if the missile was not a false alarm, and North Korea didn't shoot off a missile, who did? According to this QAnon conspiracy theory, there was a rogue CIA submarine (yes, you read that right) lurking around Hawaii, preparing to launch a missile.

It's said that QAnon posted, "Ask yourself, if a missile was launched by rogue actors, what would be the purpose? The purpose would be to create a false flag attack where blame would be pinned on a credible state actor capable of launching a ballistic missile that could hit Hawaii: North Korea. The 'rogue actors' really responsible for the attack, would thereby have created a scenario where the U.S. military would have been forced to respond."

So, if the CIA took a submarine and launched a missile, what happened? According to QAnon, the U.S. military successfully shot the missile down over the ocean, thereby averting disaster. According to this conspiracy theory, Trump knew all about it, and those around him were shocked that he did not immediately order a retaliatory strike at the supposed origin of the missile.

According to this conspiracy theory, the point of the whole ordeal was to make Trump think North Korea had lobbed a missile at Hawaii and then goad him into attacking the rogue nation. Trump did not take the bait, however, and refused to retaliate. It was supposedly then that the deep state decided to have their media puppets create the false alarm story – and Trump made no public comment on the situation.

This is one of the wacky QAnon theories out there that has received wide circulation. QAnon frequently refers to the CIA as "Clowns in Action" or just "Clowns" for short. And in several posts Q has referred to the "clowns" taking rogue actions with a submarine to spark a war. The funny thing about all this is that it almost reads like a half-baked plot that's been stolen right out of the script for "Red October."

Anyone with a penchant for early-1990s trivia might recall that this film. It was released in 1990, right before the fall of the Soviet Union, and it dealt with a rogue Soviet submarine which defected from the Soviet government and started to carry out nefarious actions of its own accord. Is the CIA experiencing their own version of a Red October?

Saddam Hussein had a Stargate

In 2003, the United States invaded Iraq. Even from a non-conspiratorial standpoint, the reasons for this invasion are a bit murky. According to George W. Bush, this was a preemptive strike against his so-called "Axis of Evil." Bush had identified Iran, Iraq, and North Korea as the most dangerous state actors when it came to U.S. interests.

Bush's administration then went into overdrive trying to prove that Saddam had weapons of mass destruction. The evidence was lacking, but Bush hammered home the point that even though detractors were looking for a smoking gun, they should hurry up and get with the program, lest it come in the form of a mushroom cloud over New York City or some other American target.

But despite all of this fearmongering of Hussein having nuclear weapons, biological weaponry, and all manner of other weapons of mass destruction (WMD), after the troops went in, secured Iraq, and overthrew Saddam, there were no WMD anywhere to be seen. What happened to them? Did that wily Saddam flush them down the toilet at the last minute? Perhaps he chucked them through a stargate.

Yes, a stargate. After Saddam was found to have no WMD on hand, one of the craziest theories developed for the real reason for the war was this loony bit about Saddam having a stargate – a portal to another world – right in his own backyard. Iraq, after all, is an interesting place with a lot of history. In fact, it was the place where recorded human history began.

Ancient Mesopotamia is the source of our oldest known human writings. And if you believe the likes of ancient astronaut guru Zecharia Sitchin, these ancient records hold some starting details about visitors from beyond. These visitors supposedly instructed ancient Iraqis (Mesopotamians) about all manner of advanced technology, and one of the things they taught these ancient people about was stargates.

According to legend, these gates were used by a group of extraterrestrial beings (the ancients called them gods) known as the "Anunnaki" who put them in place so they could easily transport themselves (and whatever else they wished to bring with them, such as WMD, perhaps) from their home world of Nibiru to ancient Iraq.

Although skeptics would tell you that all the strange myths and legends recorded in the ancient writings of Mesopotamia were just that – myths and legends – Sitchin and other ancient astronaut theorists beg to differ. They do not think it was all just an early form of science fiction; they feel that what the ancients documented was science fact. For the ancient Mesopotamians, what they wrote was about real-life events, and therefore, stargates are real.

And as for Saddam's stargate? Well, according to legend, the world's last functioning stargate could be found buried under the dust of the ancient Mesopotamian city of Nasiriyah, some 225 miles south of Baghdad. The structure supposedly sits on top of an ancient ziggurat (a Mesopotamian-styled step pyramid). But even though the stargate was intact, no one apparently knew quite how to use it.

Nevertheless, Saddam, not wanting to share his stargate (the big baby), supposedly moved it to an underground cave system in order to hide it from the rest of the world. The theory goes that the United States got sick of Saddam hiding this gem from them so they launched a war to get the stargate for themselves. Nope, it wasn't over WMD, it wasn't even over oil – the war in Iraq was over having the privilege of hopping into a stargate to say hi to the folks on Nibiru!

More specifically, the theorists contend that the war was over fear of what Saddam might do with the stargate himself. According to this conspiracy theory, Saddam had been working very hard to restore the ruined temple complex where the stargate had been found, and had poured a ton of research into the stargate to see if he could figure out how to get it up and running again. This was supposedly Saddam's own secret little Manhattan Project in the works.

As the theory goes, around 2003, Saddam's team of scientists made some kind of breakthrough and was on the verge of making the stargate operational. This is supposedly what triggered the

United States to come down on him like a ton of bricks.

Even if you were to entertain the possibility that this wild conspiracy theory is true, common sense would tell you that Saddam must not have gotten the stargate fully up and running by the time of the invasion, because if he had a working stargate, wouldn't he have stepped through it? Rather than being found cooped up in a dirty hole in the ground?

Another weird aspect of this story is the claim that the destruction of the Space Shuttle *Columbia* is somehow related to all this. You may recall that in 2003, right on the eve of the Iraq war, the Space Shuttle *Columbia* disintegrated upon re-entry into Earth's atmosphere. The shuttle was destroyed and all the astronauts on board died.

Well, guess what? Those who believe that Saddam had at least a partially functioning stargate suggest that it was the dictator's ET buddies who had somehow shot the shuttle down. After the tragedy, a defiant Saddam did indeed gloat a little bit, declaring that God had punished the Americans. Or did he mean to say that the Anunnaki had punished them?

The Founding Father Who May Have Been a Double Agent

History knows Benjamin Franklin as a brilliant diplomat and thinker – and ultimately, a founding father of the United States of America. He was also an ingenious inventor, an avid writer, and an all-around good guy that all Americans should respect and admire. Or so we have been told.

But what most do not realize is that Franklin was also a master of subterfuge and espionage. Yes, call him the James Bond of his day – Benjamin Franklin took part in many clandestine missions on behalf of various handlers. Franklin served in many crucial roles in the early United States, serving at various times as Postmaster General and Clerk of the Pennsylvania Assembly. But he also served as the colonial agent in London for Massachusetts, Pennsylvania, and Georgia.

These multiple roles created a vast network of contacts that Franklin would be able to tap into throughout his career. In 1775, on the eve of revolution, Benjamin Franklin decided to throw his lot in with the revolutionaries, resulting in his intimate participation in the creation of the "Declaration of Independence." Yet it was also during this time that he started working as a spy, for it was Franklin who established the so-called "Committee of Secret Correspondence."

This committee was established to gain intel from American-friendly operatives in Britain and other European nations. It was through this network that Benjamin the spymaster came across a man by the name of Julien Alexandre Achard de Bonvouloir. Julien was a European arms dealer who wanted to sell weapons to the United States. The cash-strapped Americans certainly could use some firepower, so this was certainly not an opportunity they would have passed up.

But looks are often deceiving. It turns out that de Bonvouloir was not being completely truthful about his background. In reality, it was all a ruse, and de Bonvouloir was a special intelligence operative working for France. He had been tasked with infiltrating the Americans by the French Foreign Minister Charles Gravier, Comte de Vergennes. De Bonvouloir then confided with Franklin that it was the intent of the French to aid the Americans against the British. Seeing a golden opportunity, Franklin didn't hesitate to lend his ear. He also gave him quite a mouthful.

He began to embellish just how potent the military strength of America was, and laid things on as thick as possible in the hopes that the French would come out on the side of the United States. He was ultimately successful in these aims, and the French did indeed eventually enter a formal alliance with the United States.

At the very same time he was engaged with the French, Franklin was also frequently hopping across the English Channel to attend the notorious Hellfire Club in England. Here, he would run into British double and even triple agents and have great concourse with them as well. In this topsy-turvy world of espionage, many of Franklin's

American associates had a hard time keeping up. Many questioned Franklin's loyalty and at times wondered whether he was their spy, or if he was spying on them. But at the end of the day, what really mattered was that Benjamin Franklin got results.

Nevertheless, other founding fathers still may have had their reservations, even after the war was over. Perhaps this is the reason why this founding father never became president. His face graces the front of the $100 bill, but he wasn't quite trusted enough to sit in the oval office. Franklin was a man of many hats, and history is still trying to figure him out.

The Advanced Aerospace Threat Identification Program

For whatever reason, the New York Times has a long history of being on the forefront when it comes to publishing bombshell material as it pertains to the possibility of alien life. It was the New York Times, after all, that published the findings of the Brookings Report in 1960, which first suggested to the public the possibility of such things, while simultaneously recommending that such details be withheld from them in the name of national security.

Flash forward to December 16th, 2017, when the New York Times randomly dropped a story called

"Glowing Auras and 'Black Money': The Pentagon's Mysterious UFO Program." Right when everyone was distracted by the Christmas holidays and the latest outrageous thing that President Trump said, the New York Times printed this bizarre story about how the U.S. government has been secretly studying UFOs since 2007.

For five whole years, from 2007 to 2012, this program regularly siphoned off 22 million dollars from the annual budget in order to investigate a phenomenon most of us thought didn't exist. This was apparently done at the behest of former Nevada Senator Harry Reid, and billionaire researcher Robert Bigelow. Even after official funding ended, it's now been disclosed that the research continued – and as far as anyone can tell, continues in some form to this very day. For what? What's out there that has piqued the Pentagon's interest?

The U.S. military has apparently encountered some pretty strange things in recent years that can't be readily explained. One of the most famous of these encounters occurred in 2004, and was captured on both video and radar. Known as the "Tic Tac" UFO, this craft seems to defy physics as it moves at extraordinary speeds, only to turn and stop on a dime. You can also hear the stunned reactions of the pilots as they try to track the fast-moving craft. At one point one shouts, "What the hell is that?"[3]

You can hear the fear and uncertainty in the pilot's voice. The audio portion is almost more convincing than the video, since the sound of a seasoned pilot being spooked like this is compelling in and of itself. The encounters had been leaked a few years prior to the 2017 revelation, but as is always the case, one never knows what to believe when it comes to UFOs. Could they have been faked? Was it a hoax of some sort?

Well, it took the Pentagon getting involved to dispel the notion that they were fakes. Because that's exactly what happened: the Pentagon, for whatever reason, felt it was necessary to confirm that the videos are real. In 2020, the Pentagon issued a statement through their official spokesperson Susan Gough to announce that the objects on the video were authentic, and remain unidentified – in other words, they are bona fide UFOs.

The idea that the Pentagon would even bother to weigh in and confirm that videos showing purported UFOs are real is strange in and of itself.

In previous decades, the Pentagon tended to debunk UFO stories, not validate them. So what gives? Why would they even bother? It seems that

---

[3] https://www.youtube.com/watch?v=uXmQHwmNa_4

the Pentagon has been doing some pretty heavy research into this field. In January of 2019, the world figured out what some of that research entailed when on January 16th of that year, at the behest of a Freedom of Information Act request, the Defense Intelligence Agency revealed 38 research programs that had been conducted. Among other things, the Pentagon was interested in "traversable wormholes, stargates, negative energy, and invisibility cloaking."[4]

These revelations are so strange, it's hard to believe them even upon hearing it straight from the horse's mouth. The most stunning revelation by far then came in the summer of 2020 when the New York Times dropped another story indicating that the Pentagon had off-world vehicles in its possession. It did so by way of reporting on the claims of an astrophysicist named Eric W. Davis, who stated that certain debris recovered had convinced him that "We couldn't make it ourselves."[5]

He then went on to suggest that he had briefed officials about off-world vehicles not made on this Earth. The New York Times then ran a few words from the former Senator from Nevada, Harry Reid, making it seem that he confirmed what this

---

[4] https://nypost.com/2019/01/24/declassified-documents-reveal-the-pentagon-investigated-ufos/?utm=newsbreak
[5] https://nerdist.com/article/pentagon-identified-ufos/

physicist had said. "Off-world," of course, can only mean one thing – that whatever these craft are, they belong to denizens from another planet. For many, this seemed to be a final confirmation that not only UFOs, but also aliens, are in fact real.

But not so fast, folks, because just a few days later, the New York Times issued a retraction stating that they had misquoted the main source of their information: former Senator Harry Reid. Initially, Reid was quoted as saying that he "believed that crashes of vehicles from other worlds *had occurred* and that retrieved materials *had been studied* secretly for decades."[6]

The New York Times then revised this to read, "[Harry Reid] believed that crashes of objects of unknown origin *may* have occurred and that retrieved materials *should* be studied."[7] If you will notice where I put my italics in the before and after quotes, you will understand why this slight alteration made such a big difference. Initially, the NYT portrayed Senator Reid as saying that crashes *had occurred* and that the crashed UFO's *had been studied*.

The revision then changed Reid's sentiments to being that he thought that UFO crashes *may have*

---

6 https://www.nytimes.com/2020/07/23/us/politics/pentagon-ufo-harry-reid-navy.html
7https://www.nytimes.com/2020/07/26/pageoneplus/correctio ns-july-25-2020.html

occurred. And in the odd chance that they had, that they *should be studied.* Reid went from confirmation of an event, to just wistfully thinking that such things may have happened and if so, they should be looked into. In other words, the UFO saga went back into the shadows once again, and still can neither be confirmed nor denied.

Interestingly, this is not the first time that a newspaper has had to walk back a seeming disclosure about the authenticity of UFOs. The infamous Roswell crash of 1947 saw a similar retraction. A few days after whatever it was crashed on a ranch in Roswell, New Mexico, a newspaper actually came out with the headline "RAAF Captures Flying Saucer on Ranch in Roswell Region."

This was apparently smoking-gun evidence that flying saucers and little green men were real, all the way back in 1947. But then the very next day, after consulting with the military, the papers corrected themselves with headlines such as "General Ramey Says Disk is a Weather Balloon" and "Ramey Says Excitement is Not Justified." So, when your UFO becomes a weather balloon do you still believe? Maybe that's a conspiracy in itself.

The Freemasons and Good Old G.A.O.T.U.

The Freemasons have had secrecy swirling around them since their founding as an official order in the 18th century. On the surface, the group just seems like a kind of club where people meet, hang out, and occasionally do charitable good works for the community. Masons themselves will tell you there's really not much to the organization; it's just a place where they go to unwind and shoot the breeze with likeminded people.

But if this so-called "club" was just a place to hang out, why even bother? I mean, you could hang out in a lot of places: coffee shops, pubs, the YMCA – so why spend all your time at a Masonic lodge? Also, if it's not that big of a deal, why pay money to be a member? Yes, every good Mason does pay his dues every year in order to stay in good standing with the group. If it's not a big deal, why do all of that?

No matter how many times Freemasons tell you that there's nothing to their organization, a strange veil still seems to be affixed between members and those on the outside. I say this from personal experience, because this writer has relatives who are Freemasons. And yet, I can't get any in-depth information from them about it. I used to ask questions, but would usually just get the runaround about Freemasonry just being a place for guys to hang out.

I can remember on one occasion pestering one of my relatives about the matter a little too much, and having the guy finally snap, "We're Satanists, all right? We worship Lucifer! Is that what you want to know?" Talk about an awkward Thanksgiving! My flustered family member was joking, of course – but there are those who really do believe that the Masons are intimately linked with the occult.

Even though the Masons don't officially view themselves as a religious organization, they are undeniably quasi-religious in nature. This is most demonstrated by the fact that the group bars atheists from joining. Yes, in order to be a member, it is required that you affirm belief in God. The Masons are not concerned with which variation of God you might believe in; you could be a Jew, Christian, Muslim, or Hindu – but you must confirm your belief in a higher power.

It might seem all well and good that the Masons are so accepting of other religions, but it still begs the question, why is there a religious requirement at all? Why does it matter whether one believes in God or not? This goes back to the Freemason notion of there being a G.A.O.T.U. involved in all things. What's the G.A.O.T.U.? Why, the Great Architect of the Universe, of course.

The term was first officially adopted by Freemasons in the early 1700s in order to describe their belief in a grand creator of the cosmos. It's generally believed that this vague designation of deity was made in order to prevent strife between members of differing religious faiths. But conspiracy theorists have proposed a darker reality to what's going on behind lodge doors. According to some theorists, the mysterious G.A.O.T.U. that Mason literature refers to is none other than Lucifer. I guess my family member was telling the truth after all, right?

But according to this conspiracy theory, Lucifer is not the same dude depicted in most Christian literature. According to this theory, Masons believe that Lucifer is the "good guy" in the cosmic struggle for humanity. For them, Lucifer is the supreme architect who created the universe, but was then hijacked by a lesser power which then presented itself as God, when in reality, Lucifer was. In many ways, such a strange and complicated belief is reminiscent of what the Gnostic Christians taught. The Gnostics believed that the God of the Old Testament was an evil usurper, whereas the God of the New Testament was the God of love and peace.

It's interesting to note that many believe that the Freemasons have their origins in an order of crusading knights from the Middle Ages known as the "Knights Templar." The Knights Templar may very well have come across Gnostic texts while excavating the Temple Mount, or as they called it, "Solomon's Temple," during the Crusades.

Some believe that the Templars became convinced that the Gnostics were right and began incorporating their teachings into the order. It would then make a whole lot of sense in light of what ultimately happened to the Knights Templar, because after three hundred years of being the number-one fighting force of Christendom, in the 1300s the Knights were suddenly arrested and charged with blasphemy. Many of these charges included accusations of satanism.

Was it a convoluted belief in Gnosticism that led to these charges? One can only wonder. At any rate, according to some conspiracy theories, once a Mason reaches a certain high ranking, they are informed of who or what the G.A.O.T.U. is – and then told not to speak a word of it to anyone.

And as long as modern-day Masons keep quiet about it, this conspiracy theory is likely to go on. It's due to this continued wall of secrecy that conspiracy theories are so prevalent when it comes to Freemasons. Yes, when there is a lack of facts, conspiracy theory usually attempts to fill in the gaps.

Vaccine Conspiracy Theories – the Anti-Vaxxers Attack!

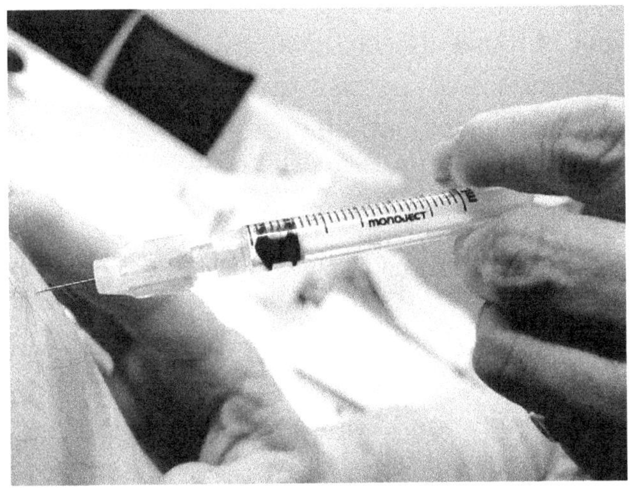

I've labeled this chapter as simply "Vaccine Conspiracy Theories" because, quite honestly, there are a lot of them out there and they branch in many different directions. There have probably been conspiracy theories made about vaccines ever since vaccines were first put into use.

All the theories do revolve around a common theme, however, of fears that the government (or whoever is in charge of distributing the vaccine) are injecting something harmful into the human body. There actually could be a small bit of real-life evidence that ignited such fears, since the early vaccines carried live viral strains and were much more dangerous than the vaccines of today, which usually contain dead viruses.

In the past, there was a low risk of someone who was inoculated becoming infected with the very thing they were being vaccinated for, but now the risk is close to zero. Yet all manner of fears and anxieties still persist over vaccines – and the consequences can be pretty dire.

This was the case on May 10th, 2008, when an entire elementary school (one that did not believe in vaccinations) had to be shut down in El Sobrante, California. The reason? There was a terrible outbreak of pertussis – otherwise known as whooping cough. This is an illness that most kids are vaccinated for, but as it turns out, this private school taught the children of some so-called anti-vaxxers (those against vaccinations) who refused to have their children vaccinated.

The anti-vaxxers have probably made the most headlines in recent years with their stance that vaccinations cause autism. This was a theory that was promoted by a former physician named Andrew Wakefield.

Wakefield proposed the theory that the widely used MMR (measles, mumps, and rubella) vaccine could be linked to the onset of autism. Wakefield introduced his supposed findings in the esteemed medical journal, *The Lancet*. If that name sounds familiar to you it should, because it's recently been at the center of the hydroxychloroquine debate.

As it turns out, its publication of Dr. Wakefield's pseudoscience was not the last time that *The Lancet* has been the source of misinformation. But at any rate, in 1998, they published Dr. Wakefield's research on vaccines. The paper had Wakefield discussing his work with 12 autistic children who had seen a deterioration in their symptoms after having been given an MMR vaccine.

These claims were later proven to be deeply flawed, and *The Lancet* eventually retracted the story. But the damage had already been done and soon, countless Americans, Europeans, and many others all across the world began to believe the conspiracy theory that the MMR vaccine led to autism. This belief then quickly evolved to include not just the MMR vaccine as a threat, but all vaccines.

As far afield as Nigeria, wild conspiracies were circulated that something as tried and true as the polio vaccine could cause AIDS or even lead to infertility. Even though these claims are patently absurd, the public opposition to vaccinations became so intense that vaccinations were stopped. The result? Polio, which had nearly been eradicated, is seeing a comeback not just in Nigeria, but also in 20 other countries.

Belief is powerful. And it seems that once people believe something strongly enough, they let their fear take over and science goes by the wayside. This, my friends, is how the anti-vaxxers as we know them today were born. At the time of writing, in the middle of the COVID-19 pandemic, the anti-vaxxers are at it again, this time insisting that it would be a grave error to take a vaccine for the coronavirus.

It's in this latest spate of anti-vaxxer conspiracy that things get really weird, because the claim that anti-vaxxers now trumpet is that the coronavirus vaccine will have a chip in it, manufactured by none other than Bill Gates, that will somehow control our bodies. Yes, it's believed that the architect of Windows is looking to create a literal window into our souls by way of a nifty new vaccine.

All I can say is that I hope that this new Microsoft vaccination suite will at least have some decent Windows updates that come along with it. But in all seriousness, this is a real belief that has made the rounds ever since the outbreak of COVID-19. It certainly creates a lot of potential for conflict and confusion if and when a vaccine is developed if half of the populace is too afraid to take it.\

And it certainly doesn't help that some rather high-profile people are bankrolling this conspiracy theory. Robert De Niro and Robert F. Kennedy Jr. are two of the most outspoken proponents for the anti-vaxx movement, and they came together back in 2017 to offer $100,000 to anyone who could prove that vaccines are safe.

The two made this offer at an anti-vaxx conference in which they decried the use of vaccines. Robert Kennedy had some of the most outspoken remarks of the evening, expressing his skepticism that physicians and the government have our best interest at heart when it comes to vaccinations.

At one point, he said, "On one hand, the government is telling pregnant women which mercury-laced fish to avoid so that they don't harm their fetuses, and on the other, the CDC supports injecting mercury-containing vaccines into pregnant women, infants and children."[8]

This is a long-running theme that Robert F. Kennedy Jr. frequently goes back to: the idea that harmful substances are in vaccines and we must use caution in their use. The public remains highly polarized over these issues and this particular conspiracy theory doesn't seem to be going away anytime soon.

---

[8] https://www.prnewswire.com/news-releases/robert-f-kennedy-jr-announces-the-world-mercury-projects-100000-challenge-with-goal-of-stopping-use-of-highly-toxic-mercury-in-vaccines-300407825.html

Plenty of Room for Conspiracy

Conspiracies are swirling around us all the time, whether we realize it or not. When there is a lack of information, or even harmful withholding of it, the mind naturally tries to fill in the blanks. We use our imagination to come up with an idea of what is really happening. It's from a lack of real data that such conspiracy theories are born. This just goes to show you just what a fine line exists between fact and fiction.

Sometimes it's simply hard to tell the difference, and it's in this netherworld limbo that the conspiracy theory resides. That's not to say that conspiracy theories can never be true – sometimes they are. But until any validation can be found, conspiracy theories remain the "choose your own adventure" of fantastical narrative.

Conspiracy theories by their nature ask the question, "What if?" What if vaccines are actually bad for you? What if a deep state runs the government? What if there's life on Mars? As long as we continue to ask questions about the official narratives we are told, there will be plenty of room for conspiracy in our lives.

Image Credits

There Really Were Witches at the Salem Witch Trial
William A. Crafts (1876) Pioneers in the settlement of America: from Florida in 1510 to California in 1849[1], Pioneers in the settlement of America: from Florida in 1510 to California in 1849. edition, Boston: Published by Samuel Walker and Company
https://commons.wikimedia.org/wiki/File:Witchcraft_at_Salem_Village.jpg

Is the Truth About Life on Mars Being Kept from Us?
European Space Agency – Own work, ESA/DLR/FU Berlin (G. Neukum),CC BY-SA 3.0 IGO
https://commons.wikimedia.org/wiki/File:Crater_Hale_in_perspective,_looking_west_ESA229685.jpg
NASA / JPL / University of Arizona – Own work, http://hirise.lpl.arizona.edu/PSP_003234_2210
https://commons.wikimedia.org/wiki/File:Face_on_Mars_with_Inset.jpg

Japan's Building a Robot Army
By user pha pha – Own work, CC BY-SA 2.0
https://www.flickr.com/photos/pha22/8264824501/

The Story of the Lost Cosmonauts
Petar Milošević - Own work, Moscow musuem of cosmonautics, CC-BY-SA-3.0
https://commons.wikimedia.org/wiki/File:Soviet_cosmonaut.JPG

Saddam Hussein had a Stargate
https://www.pikist.com/free-photo-xspmu

The Founding Father Who May Have Been a Double Agent
By user WikiImages – Own work
https://pixabay.com/photos/benjamin-franklin-1767-writer-62846/

The Advanced Aerospace Threat Identification Program
Till Krech, Uploaded by perumalism, CC-BY-2.0
https://commons.wikimedia.org/wiki/File:Berlin_mountains_with_ufo_(172884451).jpg

The Freemasons and Good Old G.A.O.T.U.
Igustavinho – Own work, CC-BY-SA-4.0
https://commons.wikimedia.org/wiki/File:Freemason-symbol-and-quote-renee-trenholm.jpg

Vaccine Conspiracy Theories – the Anti-Vaxxers Attack!
Daniel Paquet - Flu Vaccination Grippe, CC-BY-2.0
https://commons.wikimedia.org/wiki/File:Flu_Vaccination_Grippe_(5115654021).jpg